Contents

Some words are shown in bold, **like this**. You can find out what they mean by looking in the glossary.

Industrial Britain

Until the 1760s, most people in Britain lived and worked in the countryside. Many worked as farmers or did jobs at home. Over the next 150 years, new machines were invented that could make cloth and other goods much more quickly. Thousands of people moved to cities to work in the new factories.

This time is called the Industrial Revolution. Life in Britain changed in many ways. Instead of horsepower, steam was used to run new inventions such as steamships and machinery. The first railways were built. Communication was made faster with the newly invented **telegraph**. Britain sent goods around the world and became a rich and powerful nation.

CHANGING TIMES

Georgian		
	1760	Start of the Industrial Revolution
	1825	First railway (Stockton and Darlington)

	1833	Factory Act (improved working life for children)

Victorian		
	1837	Victoria becomes queen
	1837	Invention of the telegraph
	1844	Ragged Schools Union set up
	1870	Education Act
	1901	Queen Victoria dies

This is an early steam locomotive, carrying passengers.

QUEEN VICTORIA

Queen Victoria came to the throne in 1837, at the age of 18. She reigned for the next 64 years until her death in 1901. Her reign was called the Victorian period. In 1840, she married Prince Albert, her German cousin. When he died in 1861, Victoria was left heartbroken and retired from public life for many years.

What would my family be like?

If you were growing up during the Industrial Revolution, your family was probably larger than today's families. Sadly, many babies and children died at a young age from fatal diseases. In most families, your father was in charge and you were expected to do what he said.

During the Industrial Revolution, some people became very wealthy. If your family was rich, your life was very comfortable. However, life was extremely hard if your family was poor.

This painting is of a wealthy **Georgian** family.

In this workhouse laundry, boys are washing clothes.

If you came from a rich family, you probably only saw your parents in the morning and evening. You spent most of your time in the nursery where you played and slept. There, you were looked after by a **nanny** who lived with your family.

IN THE WORKHOUSE

The poorest families, who could not get jobs or support themselves, went to live in special workhouses. Conditions were terrible. Parents and children were split up. They had to do unpleasant jobs, such as crushing bones to make glue. Children had to go to the workhouse school, but they also had to do their share of work.

Where would I live?

Children from wealthy families might have two homes: a grand house in the city and a large mansion with gardens and grounds in the countryside. These houses had many rooms and expensive furniture. In a large house, you had your own nursery, bedroom, and schoolroom on the top floor. Your parents had a team of servants to do all the cooking and housework.

A wealthy **Georgian** family might have lived in grand mansion, like this one.

These terraced houses in London are back to back and crowded.

For poor children, life was very different. In cities, home might be a small, cramped **terraced** house without any garden. Your house had no running water, and you shared an outside toilet (which did not flush like modern toilets) with other people on your street. If your family was very poor, you probably all lived in one small room in a damp, dirty house. Sometimes, one room was home to several families.

WORKERS' VILLAGES

Some factory owners, such as Josiah Wedgwood (1730–1795), built houses for their workers close to their factories. Each house had two bedrooms, a kitchen, an outside toilet, and shared a water pump. Wedgwood is famous for making pottery.

What clothes would I wear?

This wealthy **Georgian** family is showing off the latest fashions.

In wealthy families, fashion was very important. Your clothes showed off how rich you were. In the 18th century, women wore elegant dresses, made from cotton or silk from India. Later, factories in Britain began to make cotton cloth, and it became more popular and affordable for ordinary people.

In Victorian times, rich women wore stiff petticoats, called crinolines, under their dresses. These made their skirts stick out in a bell shape. Later, bustles (worn under skirts to make them bunch out at the back) became popular. Men wore knee-length **frock coats** with waistcoats and top hats.

MINI ADULTS

Children from wealthy families wore smaller versions of their parents' clothes. Boys and girls wore the same type of clothes until they were about five years old. Then boys changed into short trousers, jackets, and caps. Sailor suits were very popular. Girls wore long dresses with pinafores (aprons) over the top.

Working clothes

If you were poor, you wore hand-me-downs or clothes bought from a second-hand shop. These were made from wool or cotton, patched and mended many times. Shoes were a luxury for poor people. You may have worn wooden **clogs,** but you probably went barefoot.

These children are from one of the poor areas of London.

What would I eat and drink?

Many poor families could not afford enough food to eat. Children mainly ate bread, potatoes, and **dripping**, with meat once a week. They had milk or tea to drink. They often went hungry. Some of the poorest children queued up for "**farthing** breakfasts" – a mug of cocoa and a bun – handed out by charities, such as the Salvation Army.

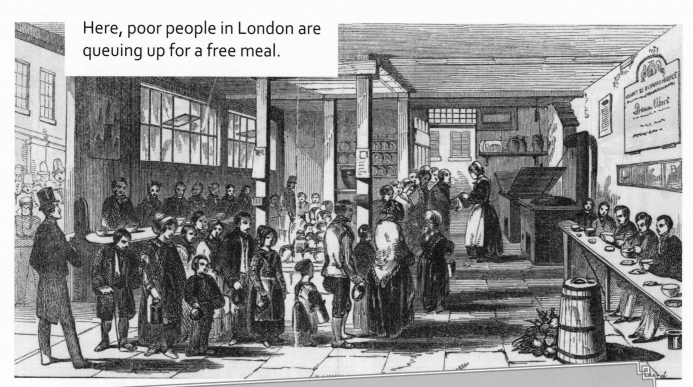

Here, poor people in London are queuing up for a free meal.

TINNED MEAT
In Victorian times, people were able to buy tinned food for the first time. This was a good way of keeping food fresh for longer. It soon became very popular because it was easy to store and cheap to buy – tinned meat was less than half the price of fresh meat.

Rich families enjoyed good food and plenty of it.

If you came from a wealthy family, you had plenty of food to eat. Children had some of their meals in the nursery, but the family also ate together in their dining room. Meal times were a chance for rich people to show off their wealth to their guests. Up to 70 different dishes might be served at a dinner party for guests to choose from. Any leftover food was given to the servants or to the poor.

Would I go to school?

At the start of the Industrial Revolution, most poor children had to go out to work and did not go to school. If you were a boy from a rich family, you were taught at home until you were 10 years old. Then, you were sent away to a **public school**, such as Eton or Harrow. There were very few schools for rich girls, so they were mostly educated at home.

Three Rs

In the classroom, children sat at long rows of desks, facing the teacher. You mainly learnt the three Rs: Reading, wRiting, and aRithemtic. If you did something wrong, your teachers might beat you with a **cane**. If you could not do your lessons, you had to sit in the corner, wearing the **dunce's cap**.

This is a school room at Harrow School.

Here, poor children are attending a Ragged School in a church hall.

The 1870 Education Act said that all children aged between five and ten must go to school, but their parents still had to pay. Schooling became free in 1891.

RAGGED SCHOOLS

Some poor children went to schools run by churches or charities. Ragged Schools were set up for poor children in the new cities and towns. Often, the classroom was a room in a house, and the older children helped to teach the younger ones.

What work would I do?

If you were poor, you went out to work from a young age to help your family. Many new jobs were created in factories and mines. The owners liked to employ children because they could be paid less than adults, usually only a few pence a week.

Some young boys worked as chimney sweeps. It was a very dirty job.

These children are
working in a coal mine.

Some children started work as young as four or five. In factories, they did jobs such as crawling under machines to pick up cotton scraps, or mending broken threads. Accidents were common and many children were badly injured. In mines, some children worked as "putters", pushing trucks of coal along tunnels. Some worked as "trappers", opening and closing trapdoors to let the trucks pass. This meant sitting alone in the dark for hours.

FACTORY ACTS

Conditions for working children were terrible. In the 1830s and 1840s, new laws were passed to improve things. These laws **banned** very young children from working in factories and mines, and limited the number of hours that they were allowed to work.

How would I have fun?

Many children worked hard, but they still liked to play. Rich children had gardens and nurseries to play in. Poor children played outside in the street. They enjoyed skipping, games such as tag and hopscotch, and playing with hoops, marbles, and balls made from old rags.

If you came from a wealthy family, you had expensive toys, such as rocking horses, dolls and dolls' houses, and toy soldiers. Reading was very popular. By the 1860s, books were being written specially for children. Books such as *Alice in Wonderland*, *Treasure Island*, and *Black Beauty* are still read today.

This picture shows children from a wealthy family playing with some of their toys.

These Victorian children are playing on the beach.

Seaside holidays

Day trips to the seaside became very popular in Victorian times. These were made possible by the railways. Some people took a week or two's holiday in summer, staying in seaside boarding houses. Children paddled in the sea, made sandcastles, and rode donkeys.

PANTO TIME

As a Christmas treat, wealthy Victorian children might go to see a pantomime, such as *Dick Whittington* or *Cinderella*. Pantos often lasted for several hours, with spectacular scenery, costumes, and many different characters. Poor children often got jobs as dancers or as part of the crowd.

What would happen if I was ill?

Towns and cities in the Industrial Revolution were dirty places to live. There were no proper **sewers** or drains, and no clean water supply. These conditions led to outbreaks of diseases such as cholera and typhoid, which killed thousands of children. Another killer was TB (tuberculosis), which spread quickly in the crowded **slums**.

This is a **Georgian** doctor with his textbooks and instruments.

At first, doctors did not understand why people got ill. Some thought that diseases were spread by bad smells or even by having wet feet! In 1854, Dr John Snow realized that some diseases, such as cholera, were carried in dirty drinking water. New sewers were built to keep water and sewage apart. This helped to cut down the number of deaths.

Doctors made many other breakthroughs. Dr Edward Jenner (1749–1823) worked out how to stop people catching smallpox by giving them a mild dose of the disease. He tried his idea out on an eight-year-old boy. This was the first vaccination.

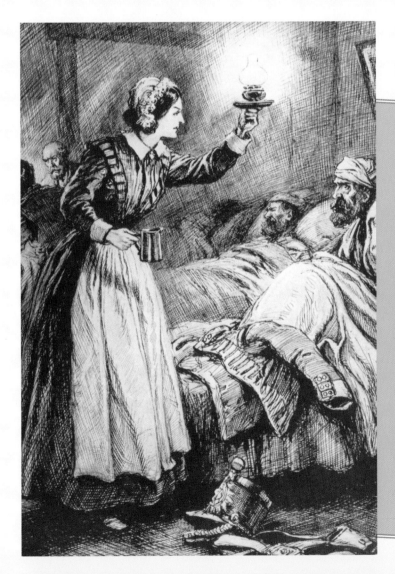

LADY WITH THE LAMP

Florence Nightingale (1820–1910) was a nurse who went to the Crimean War to look after wounded soldiers. At that time, hospitals were very dirty and many patients died. Florence quickly got busy cleaning the hospital to stop diseases from spreading, which saved lives.

What would I believe?

During the Industrial Revolution, many wealthy families went to Church of England services on Sunday and also said prayers at home. But some people thought that the Church did not care enough about the poor. They joined other Christian groups, such as the Baptists, Methodists, and Quakers. These groups worshipped in simple **chapels** and meeting houses, and helped the needy.

Many children's charities were set up in Victorian times, and some are still around today. Barnardo's was begun by Thomas Barnardo, a doctor from Ireland. In London, he was shocked to see so many children sleeping on the streets. In 1867, he set up a Ragged School (see page 15). Three years later, he opened his first home for poor boys.

In this picture, a family are crowded into their pew in church.

SUNDAY SCHOOLS

On Sundays, some poor children went to Sunday schools, run by churches. Here, they read the Bible and learnt about the Christian faith. The first Sunday school was set up by **journalist** Robert Raikes in 1780. Fifty years later, about one-quarter of children in Britain attended Sunday schools, and the largest could hold 5,000 pupils!

After the Industrial Revolution

Queen Victoria's funeral was on 28 January 1901.

On 22 January 1901, Queen Victoria died after more than 60 years on the throne. She was 81 years old. After her death, her eldest son became King Edward VII.

During the time of the Industrial Revolution, Britain and the lives of the British people changed dramatically. By 1901, the number of people in Britain had doubled. Most were now living in towns and cities, instead of in the countryside. Many people worked in mills and factories, instead of from their homes or on the land.

BRITISH EMPIRE

By the time Queen Victoria died, Britain was the most powerful country in the world. It ruled over a huge **empire**, and about one-fifth of the world's population. The British Empire included India, Australia, Canada, and large parts of Africa. **Trade** with the countries in the Empire helped to make Britain very rich.

Changing technology

Breakthroughs in technology transformed the way people travelled and communicated. At the beginning of the Industrial Revolution, people travelled by horse and horse-drawn vehicles. By the end, the railways were carrying more than a million passengers.

Isambard Kingdom Brunel was one of the greatest Victorian engineers. He worked for the Great Western Railway.

How do we know?

Many Victorian school buildings are still standing. We also have photographs of what classrooms looked like. In some museums, these classrooms have been rebuilt, so you can sit at the wooden desks. Many schools were grim places, with bare walls and high windows so that children could not look out. The teacher stood at the front of the class and wrote on the blackboard. Then the pupils copied things down and learnt them by heart.

Victorian children wrote on a writing slate instead of paper, as it could be wiped clean with a damp cloth and used again and again. A pencil made of soft slate was used to write on the hard slate, though it made a high-pitched scraping noise!

Map

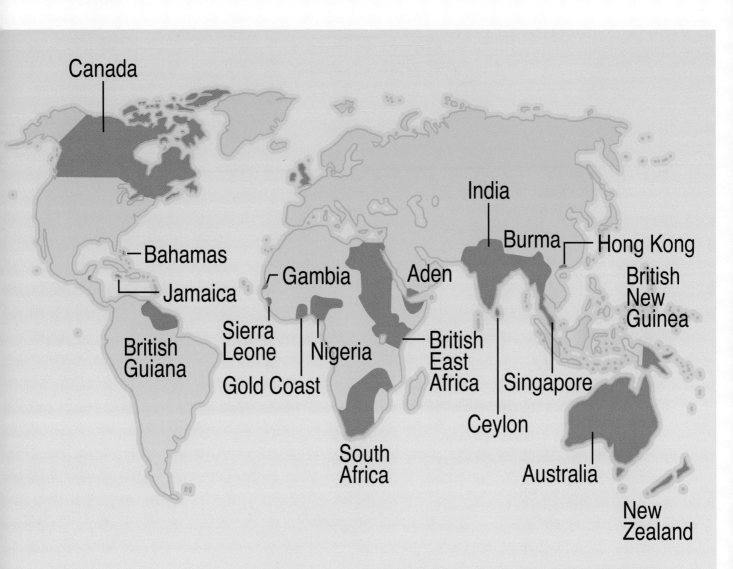

Canada

Bahamas

Jamaica

British
Guiana

Sierra
Leone

Gambia

Gold Coast

Nigeria

South
Africa

Aden

British
East
Africa

India

Burma

Ceylon

Singapore

Hong Kong

British
New
Guinea

Australia

New
Zealand

The red areas on this
map show how much of
the world was part of the
British Empire during the
Industrial Revolution.
Britain controlled roughly
20 per cent of the world's
population at the time.

Quiz

What do you know about the Industrial Revolution? Try this quiz to find out!

1. Whom did Queen Victoria marry?
   a no one
   b Prince William
   c Prince Albert

2. What was Josiah Wedgwood famous for?
   a making pottery
   b making chocolate
   c making cloth

3. What was a trapper?
   a a boy who pushed trucks in mines
   b a boy who worked trapdoors in mines
   c a boy who swept chimneys

4. How was cholera caused?
   a by bad food
   b by dirty water
   c by bad smells

5. How did people travel to the seaside?
   a by car
   b by horse
   c by train

Answers
1. c
2. a
3. b
4. b
5. c

Glossary

ban forbid

cane long, bendy stick

chapel small church or part of a church

clogs shoes made from wood, or with wooden soles

dripping fat that comes from meat when it is cooked

dunce's cap big hat with a capital D on it, to stand for "dunce", which means "stupid person"

empire group of states and territories under the rule of one country

farthing old bronze coin that was worth a quarter of an old penny

frock coat knee-length coat worn by men

Georgian period of history from 1714 to 1830

journalist person who writes articles for a newspaper

nanny person who looks after someone else's children

public school private school where parents pay for their children to go

sewer underground pipe, used to carry away human waste

slum dirty, crowded part of a city

telegraph way of sending information using radio or electrical signals

terraced one of a row of houses

trade buying and selling goods

Find out more

Books

Children in Victorian Times (Step-Up History), Jill Barber (Evans, 2011)

The Victorians in Britain (Tracking Down), Liz Gogerly (Franklin Watts, 2013)

The Vile Victorians (Horrible Histories), Terry Deary (Scholastic, 2013)

The Who's Who of the Industrial Revolution, Clive Gifford (Wayland, 2013)

Websites

www.bbc.co.uk/schools/primaryhistory/victorian_britain
This brilliant website is packed with information about children in Victorian Britain.

www.bl.uk/learning/histcitizen/georgians/georgianhome.html
These British Library web pages focus on life in Georgian times (1714–1830).

www.historylearningsite.co.uk/indrevo.htm
Find out all about the life in cities and factories during the Industrial Revolution.

resources.woodlands-junior.kent.sch.uk/homework/victorians.html
This fact-packed school website has information about Victorian times.

Places to visit

There are many sites from the time of the Industrial Revoltion to visit in Britain. You can find out about them through the following organizations:

English Heritage
www.english-heritage.org.uk

The National Trust in England, Wales, and Northern Ireland
www.nationaltrust.org.uk

The National Trust of Scotland
www.nts.org.uk

Index